(Front Cover) *The* **Lady of Mann** *resplendent in her new livery in September 1989 arrives from Heysham and makes a sprightly entry into Douglas Harbour ready for a quick turnaround prior to taking the 17.30 sailing to Dublin.* photo: Richard Danielson

(Inside front cover) *The train ferry* **Shepperton Ferry** *made her last sailing from Dover on 26th August 1972. Her place was taken by the* **Anderida** *which was equipped for the carriage of railway wagons but which had few passenger facilities. The* **Shepperton Ferry** *was then laid up in Dover's Wellington Dock and she is seen there in this panoramic view.* photo: John Hendy

(Inside back cover) *The former Isle of Wight car ferry* **Freshwater** *was bought by Western Ferries in 1985 and was renamed* **Sound of Seil** *in pursuance of their Sound of ..... nomenclature. These days, her once busy passenger accommodation is rarely used being reserved for cruises and occasional excursions when chartered for naval personnel.* photo: John Hendy

(Back cover) *The paddle steamer* **Caledonia** *(and her quasi sister, the* **Mercury**) *were the first Clyde steamers to have concealed paddleboxes. This photograph dates from early 1962 and the radar fitted in 1959 and the inflatable life rafts fitted in 1961 are clearly visible.* photo: The late R. Watson

THE
VERY BEST OF BRITISH

First in the Series

by

Richard Danielson
and
John Hendy

FERRY
Publications

ISBN 0 9513155 2 8

1830 to 1990

The Authors are delighted that this, the first in a series of favourite ferry publications, should be published in 1990 being 160 years after the date of the incorporation of the Isle of Man Steam Packet Company and the launching of its first ship, the tiny **Mona's Isle**. It gives us great pleasure to offer to the Steam Packet Company, its directors, staff, officers, seamen and women our heartiest congratulations for a very successful past and best wishes for the years ahead. We would also like to place on record, our appreciation of their confidence in us and their friendship and for their support in helping to make this book a success.

CONTENTS

Authors' Introduction . . . . Page 4

T.S.M.V. **Lady of Mann** . . . . Page 6

T.S.S. **Invicta** . . . . Page 11

T.S.M.V. **Glen Sannox** . . . . Page 17

T.S.M.V. **Free Enterprise I** . . . . Page 21

T.S.S. **Shepperton Ferry** . . . . Page 27

M.V. **Freshwater/Sound of Seil** . . . . Page 31

T.S.M.V. **Scillonian** . . . . Page 37

P.S. **Caledonia** . . . . Page 44

T.S.S. **Ben-my-Chree** . . . . Page 50

T.S.M.V. **Royal Iris** . . . . Page 57

The **Glen Sannox** was the first Clyde vessel to receive the new monastral blue livery applied to all the railway owned or controlled ships at the time. The crane with which the vessel was originally built is clearly visible but it was removed in 1972 being an obstruction and by then, surplus to requirements.

photo: John Hendy collection.

Introduction

This is the first volume of **The Very Best of British** which is a series of books covering popular passenger ferries, cross Channel boats, excursion and pleasure steamers and other similar ships.

The authors have produced more than twenty different titles in the last decade, all dedicated to specific ferries, companies or their routes. Encouraged by large numbers of enquiries for these locally based books, the authors have thereby become aware of the tremendous revival of interest in this fascinating mode of transport. As the series unfolds the authors will present a balanced mix of favourite vessels, old and new, selected from all around the coast of the British Isles.

Experience shows that many readers have, in addition to a great interest in and love of the whole subject of short-sea ships, many memories of trips aboard such vessels. Over the years, hundreds of people have written to the authors with all sorts of stories and recollections to share. Trips around the bay, crossing the Channel or Irish Sea, visits to the Clyde and Scottish Isles, the Isle of Wight and the Scillies. All these plus the once ubiquitous estuarial ferries and "skylarks" will all be immortalised in the series.

Today, the British and Continental ferry scene is dominated by great companies and equally giant ships! Ships which less then twenty years ago would have been very respectable ocean liners. The Canadian Pacific, "Empresses", Cunard's **Saxonia** and her sisters, Orient Line's **Orcades** series, Royal Mail's **Andes**, P & O's **Arcadia** and **Iberia** to name but a few, were all of smaller gross tonnage than today's modern ferries!

The title of this series is intended to highlight the best and most interesting of all short-sea ships, past and present (including ships of foreign operators) serving British ports. By its very nature this subject will cover a wide range of fascinating, popular craft.

Those ships which are British registered have to hold and display publicly a current passenger certificate before commencing any voyage carrying more than twelve passengers. Different rules apply to cargo ships and those carrying less than 12 passengers. Certificates are issued for each ship to carry a previously determined maximum number of passengers on specific voyages or classes of voyage between stated harbours. These rules are rigidly applied but dispensation is granted so that Masters can set aside certification rules in an emergency if called upon to render assistance to another ship in distress.

Principally the rules are designed to provide an adequate degree of safety for passengers and takes into account all relevant matters. These include: the nature of the ship's construction, the voyages for which the ship is intended to operate, how far from land (i.e. help) the ship is required to sail, whether the voyage is sheltered or not, stability in normal and damaged condition, buoyancy, passenger space and many others.

From the following brief descriptions readers will obtain a better idea of the intricacies of passenger ship operation:

Ships engaged on international voyages

Class I.
(P & S1)
Ships engaged on voyages (not being short international voyages) any of which are long international voyages.

Class II.
(P & S2)
Ships engaged on voyages (not being long international voyages) any of which are short international voyages.

Ships not engaged on international voyages

Class II(A). Ships engaged on voyages of any kind other than international voyages.

Class III. Ships engaged only on voyages in the course of which they are at no time more than 70 miles by sea from their point of departure and not more than 18 miles from the coast of the United Kingdom, and which are at sea only in favourable weather and during restricted periods.

Class IV. Ships engaged only on voyages in partially smooth waters, or voyages in smooth and partially smooth waters.

Class V. Ships engaged only on voyages in smooth waters.

Class VI. Ships engaged only on voyages with not more than 250 passengers on board, to sea, or in smooth or in partially smooth waters, in all cases in favourable weather and during restricted periods, in the course of which the ships are at no time more than 15 miles, exclusive of any smooth waters, from their point of departure nor more than 3 miles from land.

Class VI (A). Ships carrying not more than 50 passengers for a distance of not more than 6 miles on voyages to or from isolated communities on the islands or coast of the United Kingdom and which do not proceed for a distance or more than 3 miles from land; subject to any conditions which the Secretary of State may impose.

Note: Passenger ships often hold several different passenger certificates for the various routes they ply at different times. In this series we have quoted the principal certificates.

*21st January 1980 saw the **Ben-my-Chree** leaving Douglas into the teeth of a full south easterly gale. The autumn of the year was just as unkind and occasioned her sister ship, the **Manx Maid** to end the Ardrossan (Scotland) season on 12th September with a diversion to Greenock for the first time in memory.* photo: Richard Danielson.

*On 10th September 1989, the **Lady of Mann** is seen setting off to Dublin, whilst the **Tynwald** (ex **Antrim Princess**) is approaching Douglas from Heysham. The Steam Packet Company employ dockers all the year round to deal with mooring the roll on-roll off ships. Seasonal ropemen get the chance in the summer months to exercise their skills throwing heaving lines to the sideloaders with deadly accuracy. photo: Richard Danielson.*

Screws and bow thruster are seen here working in harmony, to bring the **Lady of Mann** *alongside the Victoria Pier, Douglas. After her rebuilding it was quite common to see the "Lady" berth, as in this view, "head out", bows to the sea. Note the mainmast/exhaust has been repainted red and black where previously it had been yellow and black except for the period immediately after her entry into service in 1976, when it was all yellow.*

photo: Richard Danielson

T.S.M.V. LADY OF MANN

Built: 1976 Builder: Ailsa Shipbuilding Company Limited, Troon.
Speed: 21 knots   Dimensions: 343' x 52'   Gross Tonnage 2,990 (prior to 1989) thereafter 3,084 tons.
Machinery: 2 x Crossley/Pielstick 12 cylinder diesels, total 11,500 bhp.
Owner/Operator: The Isle of Man Steam Packet Company Limited.

The **Lady of Mann** was the last of a quartet of purpose built drive on car ferries delivered to the Steam Packet Company in a period spanning 14 years. Her immediate predecessor, the **Mona's Queen** was also Ailsa built and diesel powered, whilst the first two of the set (**Manx Maid** and **Ben-my-Chree**) had steam turbines and came from the famous Birkenhead shipyards of Cammell Laird. The history of the **Ben-my-Chree** appears on pages 50 to 56.

Launched on 4th December 1975, fitting out of the vessel fell behind schedule and delayed delivery meant that she was not available for the motor-cycle T.T. traffic and the resulting exodus which used to call for every ship in the fleet working virtually non-stop for several days at the end of the world famous annual event.

The **Lady of Mann** has proved to be an excellent workhorse and ambassador for both the Isle of Man and the Steam Packet Company in particular. When built, she was designed to carry 1,600 passengers and about 90 cars and light vans. In furtherance of the Steam Packet policy not to mix passengers with freight none of this class of ship was built to carry heavy vehicles. They all enjoyed the side loading, ramp system that was specifically developed for them to be able to operate at almost any port or dock where the dock wall was long enough for them to put out their own portable vehicle loading ramps. The system was without its equal anywhere in the British Isles and continues to serve the Company well, running alongside the more modern method of end loading.

The ship is certainly the fastest in the present fleet and the charming description ascribed to the Company's earlier record-breakers "that their great celerity in motion is unsurpassed" applies equally to the present "Lady".

The **Lady of Mann** had only been in service for two years when a serious rival appeared on the scene in the form of the multi-purpose, roll on-roll off ship **Manx Viking.** This altered the shape of Manx shipping almost overnight and forced the Steam Packet Company to invoke their own plans for changing their operations to roll on-roll off far more quickly than if they had been left to their own devices. By 1981, all the Steam Packet freight movements were being made using their newly acquired freight ro-ro ship, the chartered **N F Jaguar** (since renamed **Peveril**) and four years later, the all year passenger service had also become handled by ro-ro ships. Two of the four side loading car ferries were withdrawn at the end of 1984 leaving only the **Lady of Mann** and the **Mona's Queen** as working examples of the class. From then onwards, they only saw rare winter service when covering for the annual overhaul of the roll on, roll off vessels.

In 1985 the Steam Packet Company and Sealink merged their Manx shipping services one result of which was that the principal mainland terminal became the Sealink owned, Port of Heysham. In the summer, the sideloaders run peak sailings to Heysham and continue to operate to the outstations namely Belfast, Dublin, Fleetwood and Liverpool. Ardrossan was abandoned at the time of the merger with Sealink and its replacement port, Stranraer only lasted four years longer before closing after the 1989 season.

During the winter of 1988/9 the *Lady of Mann* underwent major rebuilding with the intention of providing more vehicle capacity and greatly improved passenger facilities. Wright and Beyer undertook the work at Birkenhead having won the tender which went out to many major shipyards in the United Kingdom and on the Continent. More than £2,500,000 was spent and the results were little short of spectacular. Gone was the previous "ferry" image where once, maximum numbers of passengers had been carried in conditions that had become unacceptably outdated. In its place was provided comfort to the point of luxury with just 1,000 passengers now being carried on a P & S2 certificate, each in their own upholstered seat in two beautifully appointed lounges. The dining area and bar have also been rebuilt and provide efficient comfortable surroundings for their designed functions. Towards the stern of the ship, the former smokeroom and adjacent spaces have been gutted and given over to become a second car deck providing space for an additional 30 cars, also conveniently accessed from the stern spiral ramp system. In all, the *Lady of Mann* can now accommodate over 130 cars making her a highly versatile ship and she can operate or deputise on even the busiest routes.

As if to prove this, in December 1989 she was chartered by B & I Line to operate the Holyhead service whilst their ship, the chartered *Norrona* was off service. Under the command of Steam Packet Commodore, Captain Edward Fargher with Manx officers and crew, the *Lady of Mann* maintained the vital passenger link with the Irish Capital until alternative arrangements could be made. Two months later, the ship was back in action at Holyhead again. This time she was on bareboat charter to Sealink to provide cover in place of the *St. Columba* which was fire damaged and out of action.

With her new, comfortably appointed passenger areas and enlarged vehicle capacity, the future for the *Lady of Mann* looks extremely bright although she may have to go farther afield in search of the vital winter remuneration that she needs so badly to help ensure her longevity.

*This trials picture of the **Lady of Mann** shows her at full speed and her mainmast/exhaust is still painted all yellow.*
photo: Richard Danielson collection.

(Left) *On 3rd January 1981 the Irish Sea was living up to its wild reputation and as the* **Lady of Mann** *departed from Liverpool at 11.04 no one was in any doubt that the voyage would be a severe test for the ship. In fact, it turned out to be the worst by far for the whole year with her Master bringing her safely into Douglas and ringing "Finished with Engines" almost seven hours later. By way of complete contrast to the storms of 3rd January 1981, this tranquil view was taken from the* **Lady of Mann** *as she approached the Chicken Rock whilst on a Round the Island cruise on 30th August 1987.* photos: Richard Danielson.

(Above) *As part of her major rebuilding during the early part of 1989, the* **Lady of Mann** *was shot-blasted virtually all over to remove the previous 13 years of accumulated paint and rust which was estimated to weigh anything up to 100 tons.* photo: John Shepherd.

The incomparable **Invicta** *arrives at Dover on 8th August 1972 looking truly magnificent on her final sailing from Calais. photo: Andrew Jones.*

T.S.S. INVICTA

Built: 1940   Builder: Wm.Denny & Bros.Dumbarton.
Speed: 22 knots (when new)   Dimensions: 349'x 50'   Gross Tonnage 4191 tons
Fuel: Coal until 1946 refit   Oil after 1946
Machinery: Parsons steam turbine, single reduction, twin screw, Yarrow three drum water tube boilers with mechanical stoker, when coal fired.
Owners/Operators: Southern Railway Company
British Transport Commission 1st January, 1948
British Railways Board 1963
British Rail (Shipping & International Services Division) 1969

If any cross Channel steamer has been associated more with Dover than any other ship, then that honour must surely go to the third **Invicta.**

For 26 unbroken years she was in the Dover-Calais "Golden Arrow" link - that was the special service for which she was built and that was the service on which she operated until the end.

The **Invicta** was the third ship of that name to serve on the Dover-Calais route. The first was a steel paddle steamer of 1,197 gross tons, built on the Thames for the London Chatham & Dover Railway in 1882.

She was followed in 1905 by the turbine steamer **Invicta** (1,650 gross tons), built at Denny's Dumbarton yard for the South Eastern & Chatham Railway Company.

The third **Invicta** was the only British-owned turbine steamer to run in the Strait of Dover and remain on a single service.

The First Class only, all Pullman crossing had started in May 1929 with the one and only **Canterbury** but by December 1938, the Southern Railway Company were having discussions with the legendary shipbuilding yard of Wm. Denny & Bros. of Dumbarton for a larger ship. The order was duly placed the following February for delivery within fifteen months and at a contract price of £200,000.

The **Invicta** was launched into the River Leven on 14th December, 1940, having already been requisitioned by the Admiralty as an LSI (Landing Ship Infantry) but after fitting-out she sailed just a few miles down the Clyde where she remained idle for a year.

H.M.S. **Invicta** was then prepared for the ill-organised raid on Dieppe before her quiet war ended transporting thousands of troops to the Normandy beach head in June, 1944.

Later painted in the Southern's livery but still with much of her superstructure plated-in, she took up the Dover-Calais trooping run on Boxing Day 1945. The "Golden Arrow" restarted the following April when a gleaming **Canterbury** demolished austerity at a stroke but her reign in the top slot was to be brief. The **Invicta** was sent to the Tyne where, in the words of Mr. R. P. Biddle, the Southern Railway's Docks and Marine manager, she was, "stripped as bare as Mother Hubbard's cupboard", and Dover's new flagship was finally prepared for the role for which she was created.

On 15th October, 1946, under the command of Capt. H. L. Payne, the Southern's largest ship left Dover on her maiden commercial voyage and made that route her own until her demise on 8th August, 1972.

At 4,191 gross tons, the *Invicta* would be dwarfed by the ferries of the early nineties but she was, until 1966, the largest ferry to use Dover. Her extra deck, her rather heavy, imposing bow and her massive funnel, which suited her as no other could, all contributed towards the feeling of power and elegance which she engendered.

And in her Captain, the *Invicta* had a man who matched her perfectly in her larger than life proportions. Captain Payne possessed a tremendous character (and a vocabulary to match!) but was the type of man who was gifted with a Churchillian authority. Indeed, when the Prime Minister crossed the Channel, he and Captain Payne got on together like a house on fire.

To show in how much esteem he was held, Payne's protestations immediately saw the *Invicta's* bridge wing-cabs removed as he considered them "a bloody nuisance" and under his command the *Invicta* was never to berth at Folkestone, Payne declaring that his ship was far too large for the port. Gone are the days when Masters held so much power over their Marine Superintendents but Payne and the *Invicta* matched each other like horse and rider - they complemented one another perfectly.

It is difficult to appreciate in these days of intense schedules that the *Invicta* ran just one round sailing each day leaving Dover at 12.30 and arriving back five hours later. She literally became part of the town and her image remains today in a stained glass window on the south side of St. Mary's Church.

Her days were numbered when the *Horsa* arrived on station in the summer of 1972 and on a blustery 8th August, the grand old lady set off on her last passage of the Dover Strait under the command of Captain Elgar Blaxland. The "Golden Arrow", too, ended at the close of the next month. Somehow with the old girl's passing, the golden age of travel also disappeared and Dover was the poorer for it.

Later the next month, after plans to sell the ship to the Greeks failed to materialise, the *Invicta* was towed away for scrapping in Holland.

How wonderful if a new ship for Dover were to be given that special name - *Invicta* - undaunted! The only name with which to face the "Chunnel".

photo: John Hendy.

13

*Coming astern into Calais on the 27th April 1969, the power and size of the **Invicta** are shown to full advantage. Note the two black signal balls hoisted high on the mainmast warning other shipping that the vessel is navigating astern.*
photo: Andrew Jones

Here we see the **Invicta** *leaving Dover's Western Docks with the train ferry* **Twickenham Ferry** *following astern.*   *photo: Andrew Jones.*

The **Invicta** *picks up speed on leaving Dover's Western Docks and leaves the viewer in no doubt that she was one of the most majestic of such ships there has ever been.*
photo: *John Hendy.*

T.S.M.V. GLEN SANNOX

Built: 1957   Builder: Ailsa Shipbuilding Co. Ltd. Troon
Speed: 17 knots   Dimensions: 256' x 46'
Gross Tonnage: 1107 tons
Machinery: (1957) 2 x Sulzer Bros, Winterthur, 8 cylinder diesels total
*   4,400 b.h.p.*
(1977) 2 x Wichmann, Norway, 7 cylinder diesels total 4,700 b.h.p.
Owner/Operator: Caledonian Steam Packet Co. Ltd. became Caledonian
*   MacBrayne Ltd. 1973   1957/1989*
*   Hellenic Alliance S.A.   1989 to date*

When Caledonian MacBrayne disposed of the **Glen Sannox** in August 1989, one of the most versatile ferries there has ever been, left our shores for the last time.

The ship was designed specifically for the Caledonian Steam Packet Company's Arran route in those days served from both Ardrossan and Fairlie with their established rail links. The **Glen Sannox** had a Class III certificate for 1,100 passengers and in addition could carry over 40 cars, deck cargo or a mix thereof.

The original concept of vehicle carrying ferries was by no means a new one and earlier plans by the L.M.S. Railway to implement such a Clyde service had had to be shelved due to the outbreak of the War in 1939. In 1954, the first three such Clyde car ferries were delivered named **Arran, Bute** and **Cowal** (A.B.C. class). They were a great success but were quickly unable to cope with all the new traffic they generated. Therefore, it was on 30th April 1957 that Mrs. J. Ness, wife of the General Manager of British Railways (Scottish Region) performed the launching ceremony for the **Glen Sannox.** She was a larger, improved version of her A.B.C. Class predecessors.

For the next thirteen years, the **Glen Sannox** served the Isle of Arran in exemplary fashion operating up to four round trips daily. Fairlie Pier (since disused) was a good base for winter sailings and overnight layovers because it was more sheltered than Ardrossan.

The **Glen Sannox** was a state of the art, staunch seaboat and provided the Island with the best winter service it had ever had.

Unlike the earlier "ABC" vessels that had mechanically raised hoists, the one on the **Glen Sannox** was hydraulic and was too slow in operation, especially when a full load was being carried. The result was, that at peak times, the **Glen Sannox** fell further and further behind schedule and often ran well into the night to clear the backlog.

In 1964, the red Caledonian lions were applied to the funnels of the ships in the fleet - a move decided upon by the 'Caley' Company management to save any attempt by their railway masters to make them adopt the new British Railways double arrow device. However, the hulls were repainted in the so-named 'Monastral' blue the next year, in common with the other railway operated fleets.

*The **Glen Sannox** arriving at Ardrossan from Brodick (Arran) on 12th October 1986. Many would say that of all the liveries she has enjoyed in her long period of Clyde and Western Isles service, this was the most attractive.*
Photo: Ken Angus.

*Renamed **Knooz** and with her saloon windows protected by deadlights welded over them, the former **Glen Sannox** is prepared for her long delivery voyage to Greece in August 1989.*
photo: Walter Bowie.

The Scottish Transport Group was established as a result of the Transport Act 1968 for the purpose of developing and running the publicly owned Scottish bus and passenger shipping services. In 1969, railway control of the Caledonian Steam Packet Company was handed over to the Scottish Transport Group and shortly thereafter, the blue ships' hulls were repainted black again!

In May 1970, the newly acquired former Swedish ro-ro ferry **Stena Baltica** came into the Arran service with the name **Caledonia** and the **Glen Sannox** was thereby released for other duties.

The **Glen Sannox** had received a new stern ramp during her previous winter overhaul and she was thus able to start a new career, in the end serving virtually every other Clyde and Western Isle route.

In 1976 she went to Hall Russell and Co. at Aberdeen for major refurbishment in readiness for becoming the main Clyde cruising unit replacing the aged **Queen Mary**. During this operation, her twenty year old Sulzer diesel engines were replaced with Norwegian built Wichmann diesels (similar to those fitted to the Ullapool-Stornaway vessel **Suilven)** and as a result she remained the fastest postwar vessel in her fleet.

Clyde cruising suffered bad weather in the late 1970s and whilst various point-to-point sailings were offered in 1981 in place of traditional, long excursions, they were not really successful and in the end were axed.

The **Glen Sannox** was superbly versatile and found herself running out of Oban for the winter of 1977/8 and annually thereafter. Once the cruising operations came to an end, the **Glen Sannox's** principal summer operations were as general relief and stand-by ship but she was nevertheless kept quite busy. Until her sale in August 1989 she had spent up to seven winter months each remaining year on the Oban-Mull-Colonsay route.

Renamed **Knooz,** the ship left the Clyde on 9th August 1989 bound for Gibraltar to take on bunkers and then sailed onwards to Piraeus, port of Athens. Whilst in Greece, she will be altered to suit her new owners, the Hellenic Alliance SA's Red Sea pilgrim carrying service.

Laid up at Greenock receiving overhaul and general maintenance, the **Glen Sannox** is seen here on 3rd June 1985 and shows to advantage, her stern ramp and extra passenger accommodation added at various stages of her illustrious career.   photo: Richard Danielson

T.S.M.V. FREE ENTERPRISE

Built: 1962   Builder: N.V. Werf Gusto, Schiedam, Holland.
Speed: 18 knots   Dimensions: 316' x 62'   Gross Tonnage: 2,607 tons
Machinery: 2 x 12 cylinder turbo charged Smit-M.A.N. type RBL 6612
developing 3,500 s.h.p. each at 275 r.p.m.
Owners/Operators: Townsend Car Ferries Ltd. 1962/1980
*Ventouris, Greece from 1980 to date (renamed **Kimolos**)*
Ownership since transferred to Ventouris (Coast
Lines division)

The green hulled *Free Enterprise* was built to replace the converted frigate *Halladale* on the seasonal Dover - Calais car ferry service.

These were the days of seasonal tourist traffic without freight and the fact that the new ship was given a larger than usual amount of headroom on her main deck (14ft) was something of a gamble. Since the take-over of the old-established Townsend Channel Ferry by the Coventry based George Nott Industries, a far more aggressive approach had been taken to secure greater profits. The Company was sure that road freight would increase, even after their unsuccessful attempts to run the converted tank landing craft *Empire Shearwater* in a freight role during the first half of 1959.

The design of the new ship was by James Ayres, who over the years was to earn tremendous respect with his innovative work for both Townsend, and Thoresen after their merger in 1968. The *Free Enterprise* was quite revolutionary not only in her vehicle deck but also in her passenger accommodation. Open-plan lounges had not been seen before and twin funnels were the preserve of the Dunkirk train ferries.

The keel was laid on 7th August 1961 and the £1 million ship was launched by Mrs. Bernice Nott on 2nd February the following year. Her maiden voyage was due for 12th April but

in the event, the ambitious timetable was too ambitious and the new *Free Enterprise* did not sail on her Maiden Voyage until 22nd April. There were all sorts of teething problems in the first season and on one occasion, Townsend were forced to charter the French train ferry *Saint-Germain.* As can be seen from these dates, a period of just eight months elapsed between the laying of the keel and entry into service - a quite remarkable feat.

The *Free Enterprise* was capable of carrying 850 passengers and 120 cars which were driven on at the stern at both Dover and Calais. In order to save vehicles from backing all the way down the linkspans, a 22ft. turntable was provided on board in order to turn all cars (and caravans) in the correct position for easy disembarkation. In her first full season, the "Enterprise" carried some 55,000 cars (almost double that of the *Halladale* in 1961) whilst during her first full year, 83,545 cars and 250,000 passengers were transported.

In May 1965, the *Free Enterprise II* entered service, being the first British-owned drive through ferry. As the freight boom had failed to materialise, she was given what was then a traditional headroom on her main vehicle deck - plenty of room for cars but nothing much else. This was to

The Townsend Car Ferry **Free Enterprise I** *is seen here off Calais on 27th April 1969.*   photo: Andrew Jones.

The unmistakable lines of the **Free Enterprise I** *are seen here under the guise of the new name* **Kimolos** *with which she was christened when sold by Townsend to Ventouris of Piraeus, Greece in February 1980.*
photo: John Hendy.

be her undoing and within two years, when the freight started rolling, she was quite ineffective.

In preparation for the arrival of the "FE II", the pioneer **Free Enterprise** was given the suffix "I" and during her 1967 refit, an extra deck saloon was added to the sun deck, behind the funnels, thereby increasing her gross tonnage to 2607.

With Zeebrugge opened up in March 1966, the "FE I" was tried on a couple of occasions but was not a success and it was on the Calais service that she continued to impress.

The arrival of the last "Free Enterprise" series - the "FE VIII" - in 1974 saw the **Free Enterprise III** switched to Cairnryan - Larne route and in the following year, the "FE I" was tried. Neither was successful although the "FE IV" was then sent round and remained there for ten years.

With the huge new "Spirit" class now on order, the little **Free Enterprise I** completed her final sailing on Christmas Eve 1979 after which time she was sent to lay-up, pending sale, at Tilbury. Such had been the development of James Ayres' designs that the "FE I's" tiny capacity had no place in the Townsend Thoresen fleet whose latest ships were to carry as many as 350 vehicle units.

During February 1980, she was sold to Ventouris of Greece and sailed for modifications at Rotterdam as the **Kimolos**. In spite of various additions to her accommodation, the vessel was instantly recognisable as the ship on which Townsend Car Ferries had built their fortunes. A success which was sadly dashed in the dark off Zeebrugge harbour in March 1987.

Fifteen years had passed between the times that these photographs were taken. (Top) The **Free Enterprise** *enters Dover in August 1964. (Bottom) As the* **Free Enterprise I** *she comes astern into Calais in August 1979.* photos: John Hendy and Bernard McCall.

*The **Free Enterprise I** about to berth at Calais on her usual 15.00 sailing from Dover (Eastern Docks). The port's original linkspan was provided by the Company's founder, Captain S. M. Townsend, in June 1951.* *photo: John Hendy collection.*

This interesting photograph shows the **Free Enterprise I** *(nearest the camera) and the* **Free Enterprise III** *in the Granville Dock, Dover on 26th December 1979. The "F.E.I" was on her way to Tilbury to be laid up awaiting sale and the "F.E.III" later became the Isle of Man Steam Packet's unsuccessful* **Mona's Isle.**
photo: Andrew Jones.

*The train ferry **Shepperton Ferry** is seen here in May 1970 having departed from the train ferry terminal at Dover's Western Docks, with the famous Dover Castle, clearly visible on the hilltop.*
photo: Andrew Jones.

T.S.S. SHEPPERTON FERRY

Built: 1935   Builder: Swan Hunter & Wigham Richardson Ltd. Wallsend-on-Tyne
Speed: 16 knots   Dimensions: 359' x 63'   Gross Tonnage: 2,996 tons
Fuel: coal until 1947 - then heavy fuel oil
Machinery: 4 Parsons turbines, twin screw single reduction gearing, Yarrow water tube boilers
Owners/Operators: Southern Railway Company
British Transport Commission 1 January 1948
British Railways Board 1963
British Rail (Shipping & International Services Division) 1969

The coal burning steamer **Shepperton Ferry** was the last of a trio of train ferries designed by Sir Wescott Abel for the Southern Railway's Dover - Dunkirk service.

This new cross Channel link incorporated the famous "Night Ferry" through train between London and Paris which allowed passengers to climb into bed in one capital and wake up refreshed in the other.

The service was due to commence in August 1935 but problems with the specially constructed ferry dock at the western end of Dover Harbour delayed matters so that it was not until 14th October 1936 that it actually started.

The three train ferries were built at the Neptune yard of Swan Hunter & Wigham Richardson Ltd. and the "Shepperton" was delivered to her owners in March 1935. Her sisters, **Twickenham Ferry** and **Hampton Ferry** were also named after favourite crossing places of the upper Thames which were served by the Southern's suburban railway network.

Passenger accommodation was for some 500 while on the train deck, two railway lines split into four to house either twelve Wagon-Lits sleeping cars or 40, 25ft. wagons. All rolling stock had to be specially built to use both British and Continental loading gauges and upwards of 1,500 freight wagons were constructed. On the upper deck, aft, was a garage for 25 motor cars which were driven on over the side.

Under the command of Captain G.D. Walker, it was the **Shepperton Ferry** which brought home 2,500 passengers (mostly women and children) on the last commercial sailing from Dunkirk in early May 1940. The city was already being bombed and the ship was stuck in port for the two days before making for Dover. Later that summer, the "Shepperton" assisted in the evacuation of Jersey.

For most of the first months of the war, the train ferries were used as mine-layers before being sent to work as transports on the Stranraer to Larne link. This lasted until the summer of 1944 when they were converted to heavy-lift ships. Huge gantries were fitted to their sterns in order to allow lorries and railway locomotives to be lifted ashore in the French Channel ports none of which had suitable train ferry linkspans. Before the Dover - Dunkirk service restarted in December 1947 the three train ferries were converted to oil burning which made life on board just that much more bearable. In their coal burning days, the Masters wore goggles during berthing stern first at Dover, in order to prevent red-hot cinders from blinding them.

Being specialist ships on a special route, none of the train ferries saw a great deal of service elsewhere although following the loss of the car ferry **Princess Victoria** in the North Channel on the last day of January 1953, the "Hampton" became the summer vehicle ferry until the advent of the **Caledonian Princess** in December 1961.

Then during the "Caley P's" overhauls in February - March 1963 to '65, the **Shepperton Ferry** was sent north to relieve. All three train ferries had assisted at peak periods on the Dover - Boulogne car ferry route during the fifties and sixties until the arrival of the **Dover** in 1965. Wooden planking was laid across the railway lines during these periods.

Although the train ferries were quite different from anything previously seen in the Dover Strait, they were remarkably fine looking ships. Broad in the beam, but badly under-powered, they were tremendously reliable ships and all served long careers. The "Twickenham" had been sold to the Angleterre Lorraine Alsace S.A. de Navigation in September 1936 and was the first to be delivered and the last to remain in active service, not passing for scrap until her fortieth year by which time she had become the last pre-war ship in service on the English Channel.

The "Hampton" became freight only in 1969 before her sale to a subsidiary of Chandris. After lay-up at Holyhead and then Faslane, she was towed to Piraeus in July 1971. Two years later she was broken up at Valencia.

As for the **Shepperton Ferry,** she ended service on 26th August 1972 and retired to Dover's Wellington Dock before being towed to Bilbao for demolition on 12th September. Thus all three ships ended their days in Spain after a cumulative career of 116 years.

Replacements came in the form of the **Saint Eloi, Vortigern** and **Anderida** but today the Dover - Dunkirk train ferry is operated by just one ship which operates from new termini on both sides of the Channel.

With the completion of the Channel Tunnel due in May 1993, the continuing success of the train ferry on the short-sea route can be attributed to the wonderful pioneering work of the faithful **Shepperton Ferry** and her sisters.

At Berth 5 on the Admiralty Pier, Dover the **Shepperton Ferry** *is about to depart on her 17.30 sailing to Dunkirk on 4th August 1972. photo: John Hendy.*

*Gales from the south west are livening up the enclosed waters of Dover Harbour causing the smoke from the **Shepperton Ferry** to blow forward, over the wheelhouse of the ship. Without the modern luxury of stabilisers, passengers aboard this sailing could expect plenty of movement as soon as the outer breakwater was reached.*

photo: Andrew Jones.

After her sale to Western Ferries, the **Freshwater** *was renamed* **Sound of Seil** *and she is seen here in August 1989 at Hunter's Quay where Western Ferries established their linkspan to rival the Caledonian MacBrayne service from nearby Dunoon.*   photo: John Hendy.

M.V. FRESHWATER / SOUND OF SEIL

Built: 1959   Builder: Ailsa Shipbuilding Co. Ltd., Troon
Speed 10 knots Dimensions: 164' x 42'
Gross tonnage: 363 tons
Fuel: oil
Machinery: Crossley 8 cylinder two stroke engines driving two Voith Schneider propellers
Owners/Operators: British Transport Commission
British Railways Board 1963
British Rail (Shipping & International Services Division) 1969
Sealink U.K. Ltd. 1979
H.G. Pounds, Tipnor, Portsmouth 1983/1985
Anis Abiad, Lebanon 1985
Western Ferries (Clyde) Ltd. December 1985 - present
(renamed **Sound of Seil***)*

The success of the car ferries **Lymington** and **Farringford** on the Western Solent link between Lymington and Yarmouth (Isle of Wight) saw a third ship built for the half hour crossing.

The **Lymington** had pioneered Voith Schneider propulsion on her entry into service in 1938 although the post-war **Farringford** was fitted with diesel electric driven paddle wheels. With the new **Freshwater,** a return to Voith Schneider propelling units occurred and every Isle of Wight car ferry since built has been similarly fitted.

The name **Freshwater** came from the delightful paddle steamer of that name which maintained the passenger service from 1927 until her retirement in 1959. The village of Freshwater is adjacent to Yarmouth, the tourist guides claiming that it is one of the "Seven Wonders of the Isle of Wight" - Fresh water you can't drink!

The new ship entered service on 21st September 1959 and was capable of transporting 26 cars and 620 passengers.

A larger than to be expected passenger certificate was required because the Western Solent route is rail-connected at the Lymington end and a large number of foot passengers use it. In order to accommodate them, lounges were fitted below and on either side of the main vehicle deck. On the open promenade deck, above, seats were available for some 200 passengers.

The ship's design was very basic and she was really a modified punt with a central wheelhouse in order that she could be steered in both directions. Like her predecessors, the **Freshwater** was completely double ended - the positioning of the anchor denoting her bow end. Such a simple design, which by no means of the imagination could be described as "beautiful", may prompt the casual reader to ask the question, "Why on earth did the writers choose that particular ship?" Now well into her fourth decade, she is one of a number of small ferries that have done everything that has been asked of them and more - reliability personified. A work-horse certainly but as far as service goes, one of "The Very Best of British".

With the entry into service of the **Freshwater**, the **Lymington** was demoted to spare and relief ship although the summer seasons would see her as busy as ever attempting to cope with the increasing number of motorists who came to explore the Isle of Wight. This order continued unchanged until the Autumn of 1973 when the first of two new ferries for the route arrived from Robb Caledon's Dundee yard.

With the **Cenwulf** in service during mid-October, the **Farringford** was retired on 8th November, the elderly **Lymington** being withdrawn on the following day. The diesel electric paddle vessel was then switched to the Hull - New Holland crossing on which she served until the opening of the mighty Humber Bridge in June 1981. When after 1978, the **Farringford** became the only vessel on that service, the **Freshwater** had side doors cut into her vehicle deck in order that she could relieve her one time consort in 1979 and 1980.

As for the **Lymington**, she was duly sold to Western Ferries for their 20 minute crossing of the Clyde between Hunter's Quay (Dunoon) and McInroy's Point. She entered service during August 1974 and interestingly enough the **Farringford** too was sold to the same Scottish company after her service south of the border was completed. Sadly though, a change of "climate" saw her resold for scrap during 1984.

With the second new ship, the **Cenred**, entering service at Lymington in January 1974, the **Freshwater** became the summer relief and spare ship soldiering on until the end of the 1983 season after which she too was sent to lay-up pending disposal.

Her final years were to see a period of relief on the Portsmouth - Ryde route where she was anything but a success with her limited catering facilities, small lounges and lack of service speed which often meant train connections being missed. During February and March 1982, British Rail provided extra passenger accommodation by parking two old single-decker buses on deck. It was a brave gesture but neither this nor anything else provided since has matched the comfort of the much-missed **Shanklin, Southsea** and **Brading** on the Ryde passage.

The expected entry into service of Portsmouth - Fishbourne's **St. Helen** and the transfer from that service to Lymington - Yarmouth of the **Caedmon**, saw the **Freshwater** for sale and in early 1984 she was moved to the "top" of Portsmouth Harbour where she joined the line of vessels awaiting scrapping at H.G. Pounds Ltd.

The ship was eventually resold to Western Ferries (Clyde) Ltd. during December 1985 but not before she enjoyed a degree of "cloak and dagger" secrecy and a very brief sale to a Lebanese gentleman named Anis Abiad.

Mr. Abiad's intention was apparently to run the vessel on a 50 mile service between Cyprus and the Turkish mainland which seemed extremely unlikely in view of her lack of passenger facilities and also her very low freeboard for a service across the open sea. But then there came rumours that the ship was really destined for the Lebanese Christian Militia in Beirut. Whatever the truth, Mr. Abiad quickly decided that the **Freshwater** was not part of his plans and the sale to Western Ferries proceeded.

The **Freshwater** arrived at Renfrew for conversion to her new role in April 1986 during which time her ramps were replaced by doors to allow her to berth at linkspans, rather than at the concrete slipways which she had used while in the Solent. At 14.30 on 18th June, the **Freshwater**, renamed **Sound of Seil** left Hunter's Quay at the start of her new career.

*On two occasions, the **Freshwater** deputised for her former Isle of Wight fleetmate, the **Farringford** after the diesel electric paddler had moved north for service on the Humber whilst the long awaited Humber Bridge was being completed. For the journey north, the **Freshwater** was boarded up and on this occasion on 3rd January 1980, she put into Dover, with engine trouble, where she is here seen.* photo: Andrew Jones.

The ship is a little slow these days and her extra length makes her a difficult vessel to keep berthed alongside the short piers from which she works, during periods of strong winds or tides. Today, the **Sound of Seil** works with a crew of just four, five or six depending on her load and the enclosed passenger saloons are not used. Her Class V certificate permits a maximum of 400 passengers to be carried.

Occasionally, the American nuclear submarine base at Holy Loch takes her for an evening charter, at which times she proves her worth, the bar is reactivated and the accommodation is again opened-up.

In her two guises, the car ferry **Freshwater/Sound of Seil** has served the public well. Long may she continue!

*On a rainy, dark afternoon in 1973, the **Freshwater** is seen arriving at Yarmouth.*

photo: John Hendy.

A view of the **Freshwater** *leaving Lymington well loaded for Yarmouth on 24th August 1979. Note port of registry is Southampton. photo: John Hendy.*

T.S.M.V. SCILLONIAN (II)

Built: 1956   Builder: J. I. Thornycroft & Co. Ltd. Southampton
Speed: 15 knots   Dimensions: 199' x 30'
Gross Tonnage: 921 tons   Fuel: Diesel oil.
Machinery: 2 x Ruston & Hornsby diesels, each 670 bhp.
Owner/Operator: Isles of Scilly Steamship Company Ltd. 1956/1977
*P. & A. Campbell Ltd (renamed **Devonia**) 1977/1981*
*Torbay Seaways & Stevedores Ltd. (renamed **Devoniun**) 1981/1984*
*Norse Atlantic Ferries Ltd. (renamed **Syllingar**) 1984/1986*
*Hellenic Cruising Holidays, Piraeus (renamed **Remvi**) 1986 to date*

The history of the Isles of Scilly Steamship Company Limited is interesting and varied and goes back to the year 1920, although records of shipping services to the islands go back at least another century.

The sea service to the Scilly Islands is its lifeline bringing in passengers and every conceivable item needed for life in those remote communities. Exports of fresh flowers and early vegetables regularly comprised the return cargoes and this remains very much the pattern to this day. Over the years, the Company has also operated inter-island launches linking St Marys with the other main (populated) islands comprising the Scillies.

The normal service route between Penzance on the Cornish mainland to Hugh Town, capital of St. Marys used to run on 'an all year round' basis except for the mandatory overhaul, survey and dry-docking carried out each year. These days, a cargo only service runs in winter and the *Scillonian III* is laid up. Occasionally through stress of weather the service has had to divert to Newlyn, St. Ives or Falmouth but it must be said that all the Scilly ships have been particularly hardy specimens and well capable of the daily trip twenty-five miles out into the Atlantic.

The Company also operates aircraft services to the islands and has spoken of introducing a new, high speed craft. Over the years, they have also considered leaving Penzance and transferring their service elsewhere. Both Gweek and Falmouth have been suggested as places where they would be better looked after.

In 1953, it was announced by the company that they had placed an order with J. I. Thornycroft & Co. Ltd. of Woolston, Southampton for the building of a new, large passenger and cargo vessel.

Thus it was that the new ship, aptly named *Scillonian* (II) was launched on 15th November 1955 by the Duchess of Gloucester and was completed in readiness for her to commence sailings from Penzance on 28th March 1956.

Costing over £250,000, the *Scillonian* was larger, faster and generally far superior to any ship that had served the Islands previously.

Ten years after the introduction of the *Scillonian*, a second ship was built for the Company. Named *Queen of the Isles*, she was a very useful back-up but, having been designed to assist with a building boom that never really materialised it was quickly found that she was surplus to

Three views of the **Devonia** (ex **Scillonian**) laid up at Bristol in January 1981 with the **Balmoral** alongside. Clearly the **Devonia** never lost her charming, if utilitarian, cargo boat image whilst in Campbell's ownership. photos: Richard Danielson.

(opposite page top) Seen here as Campbell's **Devonia** the former **Scillonian** sails down the River Avon direct to Lundy in 1978 looking magnificent in Campbell's traditional colour scheme of black and (what Campbells used to call French Grey) cream hull and a white funnel. photo: Richard Danielson collection.

(opposite page bottom) The **Remvi**, refitting at Ambelaki (Salamis) on 15th September 1987. Note full width accommodation being built on and vehicle side loading ramp. photo: John Hendy collection.

requirements, and after some charter work to the late, much lamented P & A Campbell Limited, was disposed of to Tonga in 1970. The **Scillonian** thereafter carried on the main service route alone.

After serving the Scilly Islands faithfully and virtually without interruption for twenty-three years, it gradually became obvious that a replacement vessel would eventually be needed. Therefore, on 31st May 1977, the **Scillonian** became redundant having been replaced by a purpose built **Scillonian III.**

Our ship the **Scillonian** (II), was barely idle being promptly bought by the famous, P & A Campbell Limited whose White Funnel Fleet was renown throughout the West and South Coasts of England. Renamed **Devonia**, she was first placed in service on the River Thames but her first season was not a success. 1978 saw her on charter to Chevron Oil in Scottish waters around Loch Kishorn but this ended in May. In her short time there the ship had run aground and had to be towed to James Lamont's at Greenock for repairs to her rudder to be carried out. At the height of the 1978 summer season the ship was in action in and around the Bristol Channel partnering Campbell's other main vessel, the **Balmoral**, but the happy spectacle of two Campbell ships in operation again was to be short lived.

The ship was then laid up and languished first at Bristol and then Avonmouth whilst her future was decided. Rumours abounded of new shipping companies coming to the area to buy the ship and start running her including a proposed liner service across the Bristol Channel from Swansea. This idea was not a new one and was not without its merits but sadly, just like the earlier plans to run a spare Townsend ferry there, the plan came to nothing.

Having been advertised for sale, the **Devonia** was sold by Campbells to Torbay Seaways for their new service to the Channel Islands from Torquay. At this time she was renamed **Devoniun** and her new service having commenced on 15th May 1982 proved to be very popular and laid the foundations for her new owner's present day success. Torbay Seaways then planned to convert their service to ro-ro operation in place of the time honoured, if time consuming, crane loading of the ship and she was therefore put on the sale list for disposal at the end of the 1984 season. Her place was planned to be taken through the acquisition of the former Clyde car ferry, the **Clansman.**

In November 1984, the **Devoniun** was sold again and set sail for Scotland where her new owners, Norse Atlantic Ferries Limited trading under the name Viking Island Ferries were to use her carrying cars, passengers and cargo between Kirkwall in the Orkney Islands, Westray and over to Scalloway in Shetland. The ship was renamed **Syllingar** (Norse for Scilly) and with the service seemingly beginning to "settle down" well, disaster struck on 10th May 1985 when crankshaft problems put the ship out of action completely. Duly repaired, the ship returned to service in June but clearly, the financial damage caused by the upset was far too severe from which the young company could recover.

By August 1985, the Company was said to have debts running into hundreds of thousands of pounds and liquidation became inevitable.

On 27th November 1985, by order of the Liquidators, the **Syllingar** was moved from Kirkwall to Greenock in readiness for a possible sale. The ship was valued by the Liquidators at £70,000 and by May the following year she had been inspected by Greek shipowners. She ran trials on 17th May 1986 and, renamed **Remvi** and registered in Piraeus, set sail for Greece that night.

The ship remains in service in the Mediterranean but has been extensively rebuilt.

*The **Scillonian** rests between voyages in Penzance harbour on two different occasions in 1969 and 1970. Note the patent Thornycroft smoke dispelling funnel. The Scilly Islands' service normally operates from the Lighthouse Pier at Penzance but occasionally weather conditions dictate a move to the more sheltered Albert Pier.*
photos: Richard Danielson.

Two views, seen alongside the Haldon Pier at Torquay in June 1984, in her period of ownership by Torbay Seaways, the former **Scillonian** *had been renamed* **Devoniun** *for their services to the Channel Isles and afternoon and evening "showboat" cruises along the Devon coast. Contemporary letters and reports of wild voyages, often running late into the night with the moon said to be "dancing about above the mainmast" suggest that the ship was considered too small for comfort for those long Channel crossings. Her massive fo'c'sle was clearly indicative of a ship built to stand the worst possible Atlantic weather that she would have encountered on the Scilly Islands' service but she would also have been very lively with all that buoyancy!*   *photos: Richard Danielson.*

*On 13th May 1986, the **Syllingar** (ex **Scillonian**, **Devonia** and **Devoniun**) is seen here at Greenock flying the Greek flag, immediately after her sale for service in the Mediterranean Sea. Judging by her general condition and shabby paintwork, she had been rather neglected during and after her period of active service in Shetland waters when her owners went into liquidation.*
photo: Richard Danielson.

P.S. CALEDONIA

Built: 1934   Builder: Wm Denny & Bros. Dumbarton
Speed: 16.75 knots (when new) 14 knots (service)
Dimensions: 230'x30' (62'over paddles)
Fuel: Coal until winter 1954/55 overhaul.   Oil after winter 1954/55
Gross Tonnage: 624 tons
Machinery: Triple expansion, diagonal, paddles, two cylindrical Navy Boilers,
7 feathering floats per paddle.
Owner/Operator: Caledonian Steam Packet Co. Ltd. 1934/1970
W.H. Arnott Young & Co. 1970/1971
Bass Charrington Ltd. 1971/1980

When this ship was delivered in readiness for her trials on 27th March, 1934, she was quite unlike anything previously seen on the Clyde. Whilst clearly she was a paddle steamer (this method of propulsion still being preferred to turbines where slower speeds and a lot of pier manoeuvring was called for), no paddle boxes were evident. Instead the paddles were concealed in continuous sponsons at deck level, with just a neat white box showing on top of the paddles. A cruiser stern, slightly dumpy funnel, foremast, mainmast, high bridge, and plenty of beam all combined to give the vessel a modern, rather heavier appearance than her predecessors. The effect was quite pleasing to the eye and the **Caledonia** made no attempt to hide her "all year round, go anywhere" suitability.

In fact the ship had been built specifically to be able to maintain the often rough Ardrossan-Arran (Brodick) service in winter for which work she required a Class IIA certificate and could carry 801 passengers accordingly. In the summer months between 1st April and 31st October (or Easter if earlier than 1st April) the ship could carry 963 on her Class III certificate, whilst 1129 (Class IV) and 1300 (Class V) could

originally be accommodated when sailing in partially smooth and smooth water respectively. Later, and with extra life rafts added, the **Caledonia** was able to carry up to 1766 passengers, making light work of crowd moving on the Gourock-Dunoon and Wemyss Bay-Rothesay ferry runs.

While still a young ship the **Caledonia** was called up in 1939 for war service as a paddle minesweeper (J.125) together with her near sister the **Mercury** which sank on Christmas Day, 1940 having struck a mine. The **Caledonia** had come to the **Mercury's** aid and towed her valiantly for several hours before her sister finally slipped under the waves.

Two years later the **Caledonia** became an auxiliary anti-aircraft vessel and during the war she was named H.M.S. **Goatfell.**

She returned to peacetime duty and after extensive refitting by her builders in early 1946, she ran trials and was found to be still capable of speeds in excess of 16 knots. The **Caledonia** remained a coal burner until the winter of 1954/55 by which time she was in urgent need of re-boiling. Ailsa Shipbuilding at Troon, Scotland, successfully carried out the major task which, in the end, cost as much as the whole ship had when originally built, twenty years earlier! Once converted to burn oil fuel, she steamed better than ever and smoke, smuts and ash were thereafter (almost) able to be completely forgotten.

As the years went by, the Caledonian Steam Packet Company began to rationalise their operations and cruising gradually became less important than the direct ferry sailings. The Beeching "axe" was to be felt almost as sharply on the railway operated shipping routes as on the train services themselves with the result that ships and routes began to disappear rapidly.

In 1959 radar was fitted to the *Caledonia* - an aid to navigation that today's seafarers take for granted, whilst three years previously her tearoom became a cafeteria.

In 1969 the *Caledonia* really excelled herself taking on the rival MacBrayne mail service to Tarbert whilst their own ship, the *Lochnevis,* was out of action. She did the same later in the year when the Caledonian Steam Packet Company and David MacBrayne services were rationalised, leaving the Caledonian company with sole responsibility for the prestigious route. It speaks volumes for this wonderful old workhorse that, at the age of 35 years, she was considered best for the job! She finished this service on 8th October, 1969, and then sailed up the Clyde to be finally laid-up at Rothesay Dock, Clydebank, to await her fate.

W. H. Arnott Young and Co. bought the *Caledonia* on 11th February, 1970 and she was towed to their base at Dalmuir for possible onward sale.

Renamed *Old Caledonia* in April, 1970, to free the name for a new car ferry, the *Caledonia* was finally sold to Bass Charrington and was towed to a mooring just above Waterloo Bridge on the Thames, for use as a floating restaurant, pub and nightclub. In this role, she opened for business in May, 1972, resplendent in her fine new brewery livery and thence traded successfully for eight years in the heart of London, serving tourists and city folk alike.

Her tragic end came dramatically, early in the morning of 26th April, 1980, when she was gutted by fire and on 30th July the vessel was towed away to Milton Creek, near Sittingbourne, Kent for scrapping.

The **Caledonia** leaves Dunoon at 11.05 bound for Craigendoran on 5th August 1969.   photo: John Hendy collection.

The paddle steamer **Caledonia** *leaves Brodick (Arran) with a magnificent smoke trail in 1963 and is captured here on film having just left the berth which is in front of the Douglas Hotel, once famous for its part in the television submarine series, The Perishers.* *photo: Neil Pitts.*

The **Caledonia** *is seen here on the Thames on 9th April 1974 having been refitted as Bass Charrington's floating pub/restaurant, named* **Old Caledonia.** *It was here that she was gutted by fire on 26th April 1980.* *photo: Richard Danielson.*

The paddle steamer **Caledonia** *makes a marvellous sight at Glasgow on 14th September 1969 preparing for her final public Bridge Wharf sailing.*
photo: Andrew Jones.

(right) *The paddle steamer* **Caledonia's** *last active season's operations was in 1969. In April that year on the first sailing to Craigendoran with one of the authors and his wife aboard on honeymoon (where else !), the ship touched bottom on her approach to the pier and a few anxious moments were spent with paddles churning vigorously before the* **Caledonia** *managed to get underway again.*

(above) *Later the same day the ship was captured on film again setting off into the sunset from Gourock.* photos: Richard Danielson.

(right) *Looking forlorn and unwanted, the* **Caledonia** *lies at Gourock on a misty, wet winter's day in 1968.*

(left) *In contrast with the previous picture, the* **Caledonia** *is seen arriving at Gourock at a good speed and in order to come alongside gently, the engines will be stopped and the paddles "kicked" briefly astern if necessary. It is a popular misconception that ships' paddles could operate independently of each other. In fact in almost all cases, the paddles were on a common shaft and powered by a single powerful engine.* photos: Richard Danielson.

After four years of uncertainty, on the evening of 16th August 1989, the former Steam Packet steam car ferry **Ben-my-Chree** *was towed away from Birkenhead Docks for scrapping at Santander in northern Spain.*
photo: Gordon Ditchfield.

*At the end of the 1984 summer season, both the steam car ferries **Ben-my-Chree** and **Manx Maid** were simultaneously withdrawn from service and subsequently sold. For two weeks in 1985, the Steam Packet Company chartered back the **Ben-my-Chree** for the hectic motor-cycle T.T. period. The vessel is seen here off Heysham (which she had never previously visited) still looking majestic despite the total lack of attention prior to her being pressed into service at short notice. Her engineers did valiant work to keep her running and at times during that fortnight, had to contend with sea water and other unmentionables in the boiler feed water!* photo: Richard Danielson.

T.S.S. BEN-MY-CHREE

Built: 1966   Builder: Cammell Laird, Birkenhead, Merseyside.
Speed: 21 knots   Dimensions: 344' x 50'
Gross Tonnage: 2,762 tons   Fuel: Heavy Fuel Oil
Machinery: Twin screw, double reduction geared, Pametrada steam turbines.
9,500 shp. Integral furnace boilers.
Owner/ Operator: The Isle of Man Steam Packet Company Limited 1966/84
Markleham Trading Ltd (on behalf of New England Development
Company,Cincinnati, U S A) 1984/1989

The ***Ben-my-Chree*** was the second of a class of four drive-on passenger car ferries built for the Isle of Man Steam Packet Company. She and her earlier sister, the ***Manx Maid*** were steam turbine powered using machinery developed over very many years and they could be fairly described as having represented the zenith of the Steam Packet ship design. The ***Ben-my-Chree*** was launched on 10th December 1985 and fitting out progressed on time to enable the new ship to run her maiden voyage five months later on 12th May. Sadly the storm clouds of industrial action were by then clearly visible and the ship's career started amid the imminent disruption associated with what became the infamous seamen's strike.

Both the ***Manx Maid*** and the ***Ben-my-Chree*** (and the ***Mona's Queen*** and ***Lady of Mann*** after them) embodied in their design, a system of spiral ramps aft enabling the ship to load and unload vehicles at virtually any pier or dock wall long enough to accommodate the ship's stern. This was the Steam Packet answer to the drive-on revolution that had taken the British ferry scene by storm and obviated the need for expensive end loading facilities at the ports and resorts which the Steam Packet ships regularly served. The ships were designed for the carriage of up to 1,400 passengers,

private cars, light vans and some loose and palletised cargo was also carried on the main car deck but no attempt was made to provide a deck strength sufficient for heavy lorries and containers. These were carried on separate cargo boats until 1985 at which time the Company started operating its first multi purpose, roll on, roll off passenger and cargo vessel, the ***Mona's Isle*** (the former Townsend Ferry ***Free Enterprise III***).

The ***Ben-my-Chree*** only managed four days' commercial steaming before the commencement of the strike. These trips comprised just three single trips across the Irish Sea together with a Round the Island inaugural cruise, a very popular affair which was a "sell-out" on Sunday 15th May. The log sheets note that during this Manx speciality, the engineers had been unable to retract the stabiliser fins - the result of which was to set up very unpleasant movement in the vessel and a permanent list. In the end, the fins were retracted using the emergency hand pumps provided for the extreme need!

At 22.00 that night, the brand new ship sailed off to Barrow to lay-up for the duration of the seamen's strike and after anchoring overnight, was safely docked at 11.35 the next morning. The strike ended on 1st July and the "Ben" was able to sail for Liverpool in readiness to re-commence her summer sailings at 10.50 next day. The "Ben" ended her first, traumatic season on Saturday 24th September 1966 and having taken the service run from Douglas to Liverpool that morning, then proceeded across the Mersey to Cammell Laird's lay-up berth. That proved to be the last sailing the ship made as a two class ship as from the beginning of 1967, all the Company's ships became one class thus ending a tradition of 136 years. Single fares for 1966 were 41/- (£2.05) First Class, whilst Second Class was 33/- (£1.65). By 1967 the new one class fare was £2.00. As with the railways of the period, the class other than First Class, was variously described as Second or Third at different times.

The *Ben-my-Chree's* life became routine sharing the principal Liverpool service with the *Manx Maid* and the latest of the post war built classic passenger ships, the *Manxman,* would normally provide the overhaul reliefs. Further afield, as the various Steam Packet destinations geared themselves up for large-scale handling of cars the *Ben-my-Chree* was to be seen at Ardrossan, Belfast, Dublin and, after she had been fitted with a bow thruster in her 1977/8 winter overhaul, Fleetwood.

Sunday 2nd September 1973 provided *Ben-my-Chree* with the first (and only) opportunity for a car ferry to visit Llandudno (although not carrying any cars). Earlier that morning, the passenger ship *Tynwald* had sailed light from Liverpool to Llandudno to take the regular sailing from the North Wales resort to Douglas leaving at 10.19. The *Ben-my-Chree* having arrived at Liverpool overnight from Douglas then took the delightful coastal sail from Liverpool to Llandudno and thence she treated her passengers to an afternoon cruise of just less than two hours' duration before returning to Liverpool at 17.18 that evening. This had been the general pattern of North Wales sailings since the sad demise of the Liverpool and North Wales Steamship Co. Ltd, when they ceased to trade at the end of the 1962 summer season.

In 1972 the Steam Packet introduced its first diesel powered passenger car ferry based on the same design principles as the two earlier ships of the class, she was named *Mona's Queen.* By 1976, the fourth such vessel was brought into service named, *Lady of Mann.* Details of the *Lady of Mann* appear on pages 6 to 10.

At the end of the following season, the passenger ferry *Tynwald* was found to have major problems with her turbines and was withdrawn from service and sold for scrapping. Happily, her magnificent triple chime steam whistle was retrieved and was later fitted to the *Ben-my-Chree* which had never been previously thus adorned.

The winter overhaul of 1977 was carried out at Manchester necessitating the ship having her masts "topped" to enable her to pass under the viaduct at Runcorn. Whilst at Manchester a steam powered bow thrust unit was fitted - thought to be unique as most are normally electric powered. Later her sistership, the *Manx Maid* was similarly equipped and thereafter it was normal to see the bow thrust compartment being pumped dry of seemingly large amounts of water.

As the years went by, holiday habits changed and gradually, the pure passenger ships were phased out leaving just the four car ferries.

At the end of the 1984 season both the steam car ferries were withdrawn from service in readiness for the start of the Company's operation of their own multi purpose ro-ro passenger ship the *Mona's Isle.* Both the *Ben-my-Chree* and the *Manx Maid* were laid up at Birkenhead and subsequently sold. The intention was for the "Ben" to be sailed under her own steam to Jacksonville, Florida where her new owners, the New England Development Company of Cincinnati had planned to use her. For the purposes of the

*These views of the **Ben-my-Chree** and her engineers at work in storms were taken in the winter of early 1984. Captain Edward Fargher (later made Commodore) was in command and Chief Engineer Don Nelson had the task of supervising the nursing of the turbines throughout the voyage to stop them racing when the seas lifted the stern of the ship out of the water.* photos: Richard Danielson.

*The handsome steam turbine powered car ferries, **Ben-my-Chree** and **Manx Maid** are seen her at 20.35 on the evening of 2nd June 1981 at berths 4 and 3 of the Victoria Pier, Douglas.*
photo: Richard Danielson.

Merchant Shipping Act 1894, the vessel was registered in the name of a "shell" British company (Markleham Trading).

Their new plans failed to materialise and apart from a brief period of work when the ship was chartered back to the Steam Packet Company for the 1985 T.T. period she remained idle until 1989. On 16th August 1989, the ship was towed away from Birkenhead by the Rea tug, **Hollygarth,** bound for the Spanish shipbreaking yard of Cantabra Metalurgica SA of Santander but rumours continue to abound that she may be resold for further, static service in the Mediterranean Sea.

Moments after her launching on 10th December 1965, tugs manoeuvre the **Ben-my-Chree** *to Cammell Lairds' fitting out berth. Note the hinges for the side doors forward, often called the Liverpool doors. These were used to allow cars to drive straight onto the vehicle deck from the Landing Stage which, because it was floating, was always at a constant height relative to the ship.*   *photo: Richard Danielson collection.*

T.S.M.V. ROYAL IRIS

Built: 1951
Speed: 11 knots
Gross Tonnage: 1,234 tons
Machinery: Diesel Electric Twin Screw
4 x Ruston & Hornsby diesels coupled to 2 x G.E.C. Metropolitan Vickers Electric
Co.Ltd. main propulsion motors. Normal horsepower 1,080 bhp using three out of
four engines to generate electricity. Maximum 1,460 bhp using all four.
Owner/Operator: Corporation of Wallasey until 1969 when responsibility for all
Mersey Ferries (Wallasey and Birkenhead) was taken over by Merseyside
Passenger Transport Executive.

Builder: Wm Denny & Bros, Dumbarton
Dimensions: 160' x 48'

The futuristic looking *Royal Iris* was launched in December 1950 having been designed for a dual role. Principally, the ship was to be able to operate the Wallasey Corporation ferry routes running all the year round from Liverpool Landing Stage to Seacombe and in the summer only, on the longer trip to the erstwhile resort of New Brighton. For her second role, the *Royal Iris* was well equipped for short cruises and in her heyday, would sail out to the Bar Lightship and back on trips lasting up to three hours. Such trips also operated as dance cruises in the evenings during the course of which, copious quantities of fried and liquid refreshments were consumed earning the *Royal Iris* the nickname "The Fish and Chip Boat".

Whilst on ferry duties, she could carry 2,296 passengers but for the longer cruises, she sailed on a Class III certificate for 1,000. These days, the *Royal Iris* is licensed to carry up to 1,200 passengers on her Class V certificate, and is the sole contribution from the old Wallasey stable to today's Mersey ferries although three have survived elsewhere in new roles. Thirty years ago, ten ferries (six from Wallasey and four from Birkenhead) were kept busy operating the various ferry routes and cruises whilst these days, just two are required

most of the time. The *Royal Iris* now only sees service at peak summer times and the service is maintained by two of the three former Birkenhead ferries with the last remaining on standby. In a lifespan that has lasted 39 years to date, the *Royal Iris's* career could fairly be described as routine.

Originally the ship was painted bright green and yellow which livery later gave way to blue and white. In 1984/85, all the ferries received a bright new red, white and blue colour scheme (which they have retained) in connection with the opening of the Liverpool Flower Festival.

In addition to her ferry and cruising role, in the mid 1980s, she was moored at Liverpool Landing Stage at lunchtimes operating as the "Quarterdeck Floating Restaurant", but sadly, this practise has now ceased. The only time when the *Royal Iris* has left the Mersey occurred in April and May 1985 when she embarked upon her trip of a lifetime to help publicise Merseyside in the South of England. With a specially appointed sea-going Master, Capt. I Metcalfe, (her own being licensed for river work only) the *Royal Iris* was boarded up for protection against high seas and set sail on 29th April, bound for London on a return trip that would take her 1,500 miles, around Land's End and up

Diesel electric propulsion was chosen for the Mersey ferry and cruise ship, the **Royal Iris** *seen here making ready to depart from Seacombe landing stage at Wallasey.*
photo: Richard Danielson.

Annual dry-docking for British passenger vessels is mandatory with certain relaxations for some classes to "come out of the water" every two years. Here the **Royal Iris** *is receiving overhaul and survey prior to commencement of the 1985 season.* photos: Gordon Ditchfield.

*This fascinating picture shows the **Royal Iris** immediately after launching being manoeuvred in the River Leven to the fitting out berth by Denny's own tug tender, the 127 passenger **The Second Snark. The Second Snark** is a most interesting vessel and is still in active service. The famous Dumbarton Rock is on the left of this picture while the River Clyde stretches out beyond.*   *photo: Glasgow University Archives.*

the English Channel. On 1st May, she called briefly at Weymouth and arrived safely at Greenwich on the Thames the next day. Three weeks later, she returned to Merseyside having accomplished her mission successfully and having had the rare privilege of London's famous Tower Bridge open for her triumphant arrival!

Over the years, many proposals have emerged with a view to curtailing or streamlining the operations of the Mersey Ferries. At almost 40 years of age, the **Royal Iris** no longer fits into the planned pattern of operations which call for only two ships in service and one in reserve. The **Royal Iris's** final sailing season will be the summer of 1990 during which, in addition to her normal duties, she will traverse the Manchester Ship Canal and will also act as tender to the visiting Cunard liner, **Queen Elizabeth 2.** The **Royal Iris** will be withdrawn at the end of 1990 at which time it is hoped that she will find exciting new employment in a static role in the proposed new Princes Dock complex.

*The **Royal Iris** is seen here on her trials prior to handing over to Wallasey Corporation to whom she was delivered on 28th April 1951. The green hull paint was later raised one strake higher as can be seen from the photograph on page 62. What a fitting tribute it would be to this "grand old lady" if, when she retires from active service on the River Mersey, her livery could be restored to the original green and yellow! photo: Glasgow University Archives.*

*Originally, the **Royal Iris** appeared from the builders with a yellow and green livery and with a large lifeboat slung from davits on each side of the vessel. Later, these lifeboats were removed leaving just a small boat aft and the vessel has had various mast configurations to enable her conform with navigation light rules prevailing from time to time. The **Royal Iris** is seen here in the Mersey in August 1965, with the Steam Packet vessels **Lady of Mann** (1) and **Snaefell** alongside the Landing Stage.* *photo: John Shepherd.*

*The great beam of the **Royal Iris** (described as weird and wonderful on more than one occasion) is shown here to full advantage as she approaches Liverpool landing stage from Wallasey. She was designed for ferry work and cruising and specifically, to make her suited to the often rough water encountered in the Mersey Estuary.*
photo: Richard Danielson.

Also available from

FERRY *Publications*

SEALINK BRITISH FERRIES TO IRELAND	£3.35
THE TOWNSEND THORESEN YEARS (2nd Edition)	£6.75
ISLE OF MAN STEAM PACKET (Volume 1)	£1.90
ISLE OF MAN STEAM PACKET (Volume 2)	£3.35
BRITISH CHANNEL ISLAND FERRIES	£1.90
HARWICH — HOOK OF HOLLAND	£3.35
THE VIKING SAGA (Cherbourg & Le Havre 1964-89)	£4.45
ONLY BRITTANY FERRIES	£4.45
P&O EUROPEAN FERRIES — THE FLEET	£1.90
SEALINK ISLE OF WIGHT	£3.35
FERRIES IN CAMERA '90 (full colour)	£5.95
THE MANXMAN STORY	£1.30
FERRY POSTCARDS Nos. 1 — 24	£3.40
FANTASIA	£2.95
SALLY LINE	£3.40
OLAU	£3.85
EARL WILLIAM	£2.95
SAINT-GERMAIN	£2.95
FISHGUARD — ROSSLARE	£3.40

All prices are quoted to include postage and packing within the U.K.
For European and Overseas orders please add a further 85p per book.
Send orders to:
FERRY PUBLICATIONS, 12 MILLFIELDS CLOSE, PENTLEPOIR,
KILGETTY, DYFED SA68 0SA

Acknowledgements

The Authors are grateful to several people for their assistance in making this book a reality. Individual photographers' names appear adjacent to their own photographs but the contributions of Andy Jones, John Shepherd (former purser of the Steam Packet ship, **King Orry**), Gordon Ditchfield, Walter Bowie and Glasgow University Archives are particularly appreciated. Thanks are also due to Miles Cowsill, our partner in Ferry Publications and to the Department of Transport, Marine Library, for their respective assistance.

Readers' Footnote

The success of this series depends on our selection of the best ferries and similar ships to feature. Readers are invited to write to the Authors at the address shown below with details of any particular vessels that they would like to see appear in future editions of the series.

Published by Ferry Publications
at P.O. Box 1, Laxey, Isle of Man.
Text origination by The DeskTop Publishing Service, Douglas
Printed by Haven Colourprint, Pembroke Dock, Dyfed